Poems
for
Time Travelers
in Love

Robert Anbian

Night Horn Books
San Francisco

ISBN: 978-0-941842-08-2

Library of Congress Control Number: 2020948197

First Printing

Some of these poems first appeared in *North Coast Review*, *Oxygen*, the electronic poetry journal, *Riflt*, and as Off the Cuff Press broadsides. Audio versions appear on the Edgetone Records poetry and jazz CD *Robert Anbian and the UFQ*, and spoken word CD *I NOT I: Poems & Stories of Robert Anbian*. The poem *Au Voyage* was originally published in *Antinostalgia* (Ruddy Duck Press 1992) and appears here in revised form. *WE 3.3* is taken from the ms. of *WE Part 3*, due to be published in 2022.

Frontispiece: postcard hand-dated 1912; photographer unknown

Night Horn Books
P.O. Box 424906
San Francisco, CA 94142
nighthornbooks@yahoo.com

Printed in the U.S.A.

Contents

Avant la peste,
le monde est beau

Wish We Were Here

Mostly, we were content being nowhere
Just a little motel by the roadside with a pool shaped
          like a kidney bean
Weightless time and peering into the crater of the sky
Watching the twin shadows of your nipples lengthen
          in the sunlight across your swimsuit
Or sweating and moaning in the stuffy aerie above
          Gertrude Rechtman's Bra & Girdle Shop
You know, on South Street,
where all the hot & horny kids used to go
Or ordering *pêche melba* at Hôtel Terminus and
          running off without paying
Who knew that doom was just around the corner?
And later in rue Grégoire,
watching the wine glasses wobble and pitch 'til they'd
          thrown themselves onto the sidewalk,
smashing themselves to glittering atoms in what
          looked like pools of dark blood
Which inexplicably enraged the waiter, who stormed
          out swearing like an avenging God
Who knew that a Parisian waiter hadn't read Sartre?

The next morning, we took a walk
In a field of yellow butterflies

Who can forget?
It felt like a good day on the Western Front
You saw me coming/ and I saw you
but we never knew/ what hit us

Loving Love Too Much

Loving love too much Laughter
Too much Sugary diphthong
On a friend's lips Fragrant
Pathway to a lover's vagrant
Kiss Slip of the tongue's hot
Warm & willowy summer
All day Loving daydreaming
The smack of Mother Mary's
Maraschino lips at playtime
Sweet song Sweet taste
Of all we want To say
Loving words
Forever & a day The
Said and the unsaid
'there is a melody
deep in my heart'
Our jukebox days
Walkabout nights

Cultural Affairs

A woman waiting in line
in Berkeley, California
said,
"I'm not a woman,
I'm a Gyno-American
"And I'm expanding
my vaginal aura,"
said she
"That
would certainly get
my vote," said me
"Thank God, I'm an atheist,"
said Luis Buñuel, while
peeling a hard-boiled egg

Everyone seems to be going a little mad
          nowadays
One world, one peace

The man   in the moon   in the tree
    and the man   the woman   in the tree
in the tree   in the tree   in the moon

The Noble Savage is dead
Long live the Noble Sausage

Long live television

"And we're all gonna be typhoons"
boom

Repeat Chorus

O Gliddia farriva
Me darlin' baleful dread,
Donut murther we

Today

Today, with the sun
in my ear
Today, the sea in my soul
Today, on the horizon,
a smudge of sincerity
Today, without a prayer
Without a paddle
Today, without a doubt

Today, the pale moon chasing us still
One almost died a hundred times!

Today, the mighty Pacific smashing itself on the rocks
So long to a lifetime of so longs!

What have we learned?
That in heaven everything is fine,
while on earth everyone likes pizza
That all the love of Siddhartha's father
could not defeat the world,
nor the Buddha his followers' following
They came trailing after, hang-dog
and needing a god-fix

Terror reminds us — once we were happy!
And truth is treason in every nation
And Eden was a place called Earth
Also,
they played Brahms at Nietzsche's funeral,
and Nietzsche hated the music of Brahms
Ah! the artistic temperament…a little abyss
on the road to happiness

Today, like nothing expected!
A maze upon the waters
Light on the deep
Waves of sparkling periphrasis
under the silent perilune
Up periscope, camerado!
Ah! periplums *in perpetuum*

Yum, Yum, Yum

Crazy as a *lune*,
       big as the sky
Set out to
       circumnavi-
       gate the globe
and ended up in
       the *zuppa*
Chunky soul soup
       in a little
       round
       bowl
Bouillabaisse de
       bête &
       hot
       mulligan
       of bones
That ol' heart-a
       mine, and
       etc.,/ oh
       savory,
       savory
       wound

Yum, Yum, Yum
The grateful prey
       turns its
       belly
       skyward
I remember
       everything!
The earth exhales
       with pure
       pleasure
The breeze at the
       end of the
       field
smells of corn and
       freshly cut
       hay

Night & Day

*I can't forget
the lilac scent,
impalement of your sweet wax*

The pendulums in your body,
moons of flesh swaying
between my rigid thighs
Radiant the mystery tide of night
that wells and carries away
my wooden corpse
Under your cool, milky gaze,
your waves of silken hair
Splendor of your wet lips
about which I had thought
so long out of time

O burnished Black giantess
leaning out of the sun
Golden breath upon my eyes
Aroma of salt, sunflowers, hot skin
flooding my head with brilliant emptiness
Nipples of small blue flames
igniting the darkness behind my teeth

Buoyant orbit of your tongue
that moistens my eyelids
and sends me sailing
out over the dawning moons
of your ineluctable buttocks

Beautiful rebel, naked soul…

Speak Also You

Sprich auch du —Paul Celan

Speak also you
Breath, word, bell
In the tower spoken
Also you by the living
Across the sunlit valley tolling
By the dead also you
Echoing in the vagabond earth
Cave, breath, word
Skull agape you also
Whistling in the hungry dawn
The winter wolves
Find your smoking heart
Lie down in ash
Lie down in clover
Sing also you, mortal psalm,
In the choiring silence

empires rise
empires fall, your
mimosa hair

The Fall

Oh God, how we smooched and clawed in the rec-
        room dank&dark
and cool of Jobim&Sinatra, sweaty backs on sticky
        couches
Slipping tongues between mashed lips
as we swore as kids never to do
Swelled-up BIG FAT cartoon LIPS!
Stumbled shell-eyed&brain-shocked into the yellow
        Jersey suburban nightmare kitchen — every-
        one was staring!
With electric halo-headed Eraserhead hair and twisty
        damp shirt&trouser Gumby torsos,
mumbling, the screen door squealing,
stepping out under the starry eon night sky
and could no longer believe in God
or ever again tell mother
she was loved above everything else
in all His Great and Fallen Universe

Civil Wars

I remember clouds of mosquitoes whining on the
        wood's edge,
millions of lightning bugs flashing in the dark corn
Crickets down by the creek rasping like breathless
        buglers...
I remember you in the back seat,
soft and damp and blacker than night
Your blueberry lips, big militant eyes
I opened your blouse, slipped my hand under your
        teenage bra,
felt the salvo beneath the warm flesh...
We were in high school, had history class together
Ah, Jefferson, *mon frère*, a regular red-haired devil...

WE 3.3

...from Harleigh Cemetery to Atlantic City,
where icy winds sang among the broken waves
and the great Ferris wheel stood frozen above the
        empty boardwalk
The beach houses were easy to break into,
and drank the booze the owners had left behind
Huddled half-naked under blankets on the porch
        swings and whispering,
chased the hot and cool spots all over our bodies until
        our fingers turned to water in the uncertain
        crevices and cascading,
flooded our loins with the acid brine of virginal sex
Listened to the growling surf, the piping sand,
and opening our hearts heard the blood singing out of
        ocean depths
Petty theft and winter nights at the beach were a world
        apart, which we shared alone together — until
        the cops showed up
Love enters all at once, camerada, and keeps entering

Carl Street

O Belladonna of the peach-blow cheeks
humming her songs and adorning her limbs
with bracelets, with cocaine, with feathers
Dancing clumsily, showing off her buttocks with
        touching naïveté
While the plummy evening flies westward over the
        Golden Gate
Soft and playful as a cherub, she tastes like warm apple
        tart
Her friend, Frodo Godot, hairy as a caveman,
dressed in top hat, tutu, and spats,
comes striding down the hall, half-tumescent penis
walloping from thigh to thigh
Everyone and everything is confused
Piaf and Zadora on the speakers, green smoke, black
        light, naked strangers starting awake in tubs
Even the beat cops stop by for a puff
Avant la peste, le monde est beau
In the middle bedroom, hearts in perpetual motion,
the lesbians never cease arguing, the dark-skinned dyke
who demands absolute loyalty, and the white-skinned
        girly one

who can't help giving it to every demanding dyke
Ah, Bella! You drink too much coca-cola,
but I'll love you madly all weekend anyway…

Six A.M.

Love will kill you
Love will blind you
Selfishness is such a burden
Shout from the window at night,
anonymous you,
over the rooftops
Make love to me
Love will make you hate
I hate to see you go
Up to your swinging ass
in sassy love,
my viral human
Open your bloody heart,
you can hear it
Open your bloody ear,
you can smell it
Eat it
It's you
Take dreams
Take hopes
Take despairs
when you go

You're still there
Take nothing,
nothing's there
but you
Then not
Nothing

Crazy Cloud Poem #1

...no big-time Buddha in the woods.
—Crazy Cloud (Ikkyū, b. 1394)

Crazy Cloud reminds us
there is no Buddha in nature
And the song of a single wren
surpasses the singing of 10,000 sutras
by 10,000 monks
So why go around in skullcap and gown,
brandishing a crooked stick
and practicing a holy look?
If you make love in the morning
and hear a songbird in the afternoon,
haven't you moved heaven and earth?
Even lost you are on the Way

She Came on Two Wheels

She came on two wheels
Sun pursued by moon
Eye of a storm chased
By the eye of a dog

She came on two wheels
Whirlwind after whirlwind
Rain after lightning
Dream after delirium

She came on two wheels
Off the plains of Kansas
Atop the double Os of Hollywood
Where her people went mad

She came on two wheels
Racing dawn, racing tomorrow
A bravery so prodigious I fell
Heels-over-head into being

She came on two wheels
I flailed madly but tumbled
Helplessly under the front tire
And under the back one too

She came on two wheels
Flying ankles, winking shadows
Glowing thighs, speckled shoulders
Billowing waves of silk

She came on two wheels
Day followed by night
Breath by breathlessness
Terror by joy

She came on two wheels
Heart pursued by soul

Above Polk Street

Darkness falls
Over the flat, two
Candles alight

Fawn-like
Complexion, wood-
Land eyes

Crowded street
Below, we mingle
Our tongues

Lamp in the garden
Your blouse opens
Two buds

Purple sky
Neon window, your
Belly a sea

Crescent moon
Across my shade, twain
Torsos aglow

Empires rise
Empires fall, your
Mimosa hair

Festival of lights
Lanterns drifting downstream
Coming to you

Four Confessions

1.
There's nothing like it
The keen whine of the insects in the tall grass
The unblinking eye of the sun
No more joking
Lie down, look skyward
I have loved you for so long
Two kites, tethered in separate countries,
Aloft in the same sky

2.
The whisper of cars on the highway at night
makes me feel naked
I lie awake listening to your breathing,
soft palms squeezing my heart

3.
Truth is the higher love
that transforms life
The host cannot survive
The heart's in the syntax

4.
Born in a cellar, feller
More monkey than man
More dog than poet
Save the juicy ones!
Man, what a mutt!

Near Guerneville

Naked on the river
Falling in love again
The light at dusk

grey sea, grey sky
we are the sublime land

Au Voyage

for Nona

1. **The Three Trees**

   After love the lovers
   babbled seamlessly —
   animals, nights, words
   de drie bomen
   the bells sounded midnight
   behind the Keizersgracht —
   light breezes, transparent darkness,
   historical musk of your full being —
   grey sea, grey sky,
   we are the sublime land —
   thief and thief,
   we are the venerated crucifixion —

2. **Night at the Modern**

   for Rolf

   A great soul wept
   into the breast
   of a marionette —

the wood is alive,
and the forest — *dangereuse!*
Ah, M. Moreau,
did you bleed paint
between one new ancientness
and another old modernity?
To St. Francis in the wood
came the beasts, furry
bosom in the form
of a broken circle —
that was a love full of silences!
O rich pauper!
In a city bearing his name,
a fragile breast awaits
full of joys and heartbeats
and one tiny, stupendous tear —

3. **Who?**

Qui était René Villermé?
Who knows? Who cares?
He's an ancient wall, a corner,
a sexual ecstasy inside the stone —
he's an artist who jumped
off the page and into
a film, and off again
into the pale lemon light —
rue René-Villermé?

I, the poet, know — I,
the yesterday and tomorrow, care —
he's the nobody
embracing the yesbody —

4. **How Long?**

How long did it take
to burn down, our 5-franc candle
in that monstrous, color-stained,
edifice of faith and time?
A touch! A furtive century!
Vistas of ascending,
broken arches —
I can't forget
the lilac scent,
impalement of your sweet wax —
O rose, flame, baptism,
liquid gold — O masses
of votive auras of primitive faces,
naïve postures — *Notre dame*
des ombres, they are ours!
Ah, spectral intercessor —
maternal gloom feathered with light —
I could've bought the 10-franc one,
but made it up
between the old nun's
quivering lip,

and the blind man's orbs
revolving outside
in the dazzling white plaza —

5. **Champ de Mars**

There is always
a bit of sadness
in love —
wrong alley, blind stair,
flowering cul-de-sac,
immovable fragrance —
tear sliding along a subway track!
Always a hesitation abandoned
for a tomorrow immolation —
a girl who buries her steaming eyes
in the nape of her boy's neck —
underground! We rise as if
the steps could not ascend
without us — always
a bit of death hovering
over the long green field.
Chère combattante, I weep
for the battle won —

6. **Gates of Hell**

So much white marble,
so many green originals!
And then, copies!
Yo, Auguste, were you
the plaything after all
of the society ladies — ?
What bronze, what stones
buried their centimes of laughter
in so much potent silence — ?
And then so many Balzacs,
and so much Balzac!

7. **Chez Père Lachaise**

> *…that giant garbage can!*
> —Jean Cocteau

Look at what grandeur has come
to rest in your quiet, lofty spot,
old father piece-of-ground —
what palatial shoulders, and dark,
haloed backs have hunkered down
in your shoulder-to-shoulder suburb —
mute cobbled paths mounting
to nowhere — chinks of light
shifting among the dark May leaves —
What secrets, old father chockablock,
could Louis have spoken to you?

Had he understood sin,
he would've left off being King
and become sooner mute —
O Héloïse et Abelard!
O Communards,
tombés dans l'air!
Nerval, penniless suicide!
Michelet, passionate tribune!
Balzac, always Balzac!
Méliès, whose horse was there,
then not, becoming a little toy —
et le 'Door,' *où va-t-il?*
Old *père* cryptic-grin,
you were teaching us all along
that death was postmodern
But we, royally naked,
went right on living —

8. **Oh!**

Oh, gypsy, don't squeeze so hard!
Gypsy, who put the steel in your fingernails
that are piercing my skin? penetrating to the heart!
Gypsy, who gave you the dusky look of the
        grave — ?
the scarf of the forever-on-the-road — ?
Gypsy, you're cutting to the bone — !
Oh, gypsy, don't suspend your baby like that,

between the fright and the crime,
the cobblestone and the spire — !
Gypsy, who gave you the voice of a knife — ?
the clamor of tattered skirts — ?
Not so hard!
Am I the one
who chased you
through forests, nights, songs,
fires, violins, rituals — ?
Am I the one
who wrote your romance
in a hail of bullets — ?
Oh, dark-eye,
am I the deep pocket,
the 50,000 lira note, the red blood drawn
by your nails of grief — ?
Oh, mother-gypsy,
not so hard — ! not so deep — !

9. **Midnight: Piazza Santa Croce**

O spectral crane
O spiritus sanctus
What fabulous engineering,
aloft in the Prussian-blue night,
could've engendered this birth
of miraculous marble —
the green which is veins,

the red which is blood,
the white which is never and forever —
out of the brown earth-stone
and fractious mists of valleys —
Goodbye Savonarola — !
old hot-breath, neither up nor down!
Calm yourself, *mio cuore*.
In the soft, bright, enfolded blue
robe, in the incised golden rays
proceeding from a white dove,
in the simple loggia of Fra Giovanni,
called "Beato" and "Angelico" —
wake up from gloom, dampened monks! —
the scene is simply set:
humbled exalted woman!
transfigured tomorrow!

10. **In Tuscany in May**

For John & Anna

In Tuscany in May
it snows even in the trains —
flakes of feathery white pollen
falling through pale yellow light —
light of the Renaissance masters
and the skin-burned farmers
who worked rolling patches
of vines and muscle and stone —

wild red poppies stain the fields!
Ochreous soaring battlements
conceal — you enter them as if
entering a petrified egg —
coolly whispering frescoes
of civic pageantry
brushing the stone ceilings
with an ardent rouge —
Outside, the sky takes wing
with the screeching and swooping
of the arrowing swallows
among the red-tiled roofs — !
among the all-night eaves
of the hidden courtyard of laughter,
shouts, amorous clatter of dishware —
like the old Italian men in the mornings
conversing in the piazzas near the banks,
or the big women sweeping in doorways,
baking the air with a warmth
of maternal shoulders —
or like the radiant young at caffé tables
with their cigarettes and natural exhibitionism —
like the burbling of the league of pigeons in the
          campo —
like the conviviality of the awed masses
who scarcely believe
the wrinkled landscape
blooming in the palms of their hands —

In Tuscany in May
it snows even in the soft,
eggshell-colored rooms,
with their warm, billowing,
precise moments of coitus
defying all the living past
and embracing every ancient future —

To Ronald F. Sauer, Man, Poet & Beast

The trouble with most poems is they're
nothing but poems. —Walt Whitman

We agree on almost everything,
so naturally we argue all the time
— whether Elvis was a narc or not,
whether Kerouac supported the war in Vietnam
or not (though we know he was more poet
than novelist, save, maybe, for *Visions of Cody*)
We argue over Rilke, whose angels give me
a pain in the ass; over Wallace Stevens,
whose highbrow Anglo Modernism
brings out the chimpanzee in me; concerning
        Rimbaud
and the East African slave trade circa the 1880s,
such fierce noise and flashing of dishware!
Ron, I wanted to tell you that you are completely mad,
and I wanna be too...
You correct my anger at Abraham over Isaac
— kick the old man in the balls and run for it! sayeth I
But you sayeth it is the heavy hand of the old God
being palsied by the holiness of humans becoming
        human

Merde alors, mon ami, you are always teaching me
that true intelligence requires generosity of spirit.
This is your gift, your gift to me
on a rainy Saturday North Beach afternoon
where I wander lost and surprised…
About Baudelaire, of course, we never disagree,
or that Ginsberg was our Whitman whatever
the poet-professors are babbling about nowadays.
Or that Ramu Aki, fugitive poet,
is one of America's great unknowns,
or that Jerry Ferraz, lover of song, poetry and cup,
is another 'banished immortal.'
We're coincidentally rereading
Tropic of Cancer and it occurs to me
you will one day be our Henry Miller, serene
in a Big Sur of the mind if not of actuality,
playing ping-pong with pleasant naked ladies,
making art, feeling "merry and bright,"
as Henry felt, saying to anyone
who'd listen that he couldn't remember
why he was so angry in the wild and scatological
books of his younger self. I say bravo for him!
Let it be inscribed in the graffitied halls
of heaven that I love all poets, and Ron Sauer best
For if the sword of Rome was Marcellus,
then surely its shield was Fabius,
who saved the Republic from Hannibal
only to have it fall one day to Caesar Augustus

Play your guitar and sing,
poets got dem ol' empire blues again
Inevitably, said Engels, more or less
Ah well, everyone needs a kick in the ol' arcane
now and again, dontcha know, smoke
a little schmoogadoo, and exist awhile
in quietude, milk, and kindness
Rebecca walks in about then
— passing in a flowing scarf
under the old arched porticos, by the glossy waters,
of her luminous collages — squinting through
the haze, saying with brazen clarity, "But
why do you think it's all so important?"
Hot damn, boy, she's got us there!
So we sit a-quiet in the Cagean calamity of traffic
drifting through the open fire escape doors
of the Columbus Ave. apartment, bejeweled with art,
like the inside of a Fabergé egg by Kandinsky,
and consider unsoberly the everlasting crack
in the quotidian collage of banal delirium cum tremens
of the "silly human parade" passing outside,
streetwise, each head a poem yearning to take off its
        hat,
revealing brilliance of mind and coolness of spirit…
We play the 1940s interrogation game,
you shine a lamp in my face, growl, "C'mon,
fess up…you want to be famous!"
"No," I say, "I want to be heard."

We switch positions, I grit my teeth, "C'mon ya mug,
admit it, you want to be loved."
"No," you say, "I want to be free."
Ah, *la risposta migliore*, because you and me,
        camerado,
we've been through those noir scenes, neighborhoods
        of fear,
prisons of wanting and needing, of self, selfhood,
        selfishness,
trying to be nobodies or everybody among so many
        somebodies...
London bridge is falling down/ and so is I
If I could answer Rebecca's beautiful question,
I'd fly away from her fire escape...
Instead, I step onto the wine-warm sidewalk,
into the flash-bang of the hum-drumming circus
of holy-shit commerce, finding myself drifting
across slow-motion streets, everybody reaching for
        something unseen,
everyone talking and no one hearing a thing,
only the din and lilt of everyday ecstasies and anxieties,
passing under the angled, rain-scuttled rooftops
of this old-world Italian hillside opera starring
old-timey ghosts and the not-yet-dead
and the remembered and the unremembered...
it's all here, all part of my great Beat epic,
I call it, "Don't Give Me No More of That Beat Shit!"
Now, damn it, Ron! Must I reread Stevens, Rilke, and

the Old Testament, too, with a more open heart?
Must I cease my relentless melancholy over Rimbaud?
Must I continue re-reading Miller, including both
    Tropics
and the entire Rosy Crucifixion, *Sexus*, *Plexus* and
    Nexus,
not forgetting *The Air-Conditioned Nightmare*
or *The Colossus of Maroussi*? Must I keep
translating Baudelaire, though I can't do better
than you or his other great translators?
Must I,
in short,
forgive
Elvis?
And the answer to these questions, and to sundry
    others
pertaining to life, love, death, and all
that Whitman called "the greater purport,"
is
yes.

Mt. Holly Days

Was life really so sweet
on Top E Toy Street
all those summers ago?
When we used to grope and kiss
down by the lake named
for the Quaker Abolitionist
(who was never as a rule
mentioned at the local high school)
all those warm Jersey summers ago — ?

When life unfolded like a poem —
trucks rumbling in the roads,
screen doors slamming closed,
kids yelling from yard to yard, dawn to dusk,
betwixt one war and the next,
shouting all together, "Camelot or bust!"
While up on the Mount,
clandestine beneath the pines,
the ducktailed boys smoked their ciggies,
and the girls with pierced ears, feeling sublime,
showed off their innocent titties
— wasn't that a dream of time
before time began to count?

2.

When we all were small
the Devil was after us —
winos lounging on the stoop
next to old man Shoop's,
where the latest Playboy would go on display,
making every schoolboy dawdle and delay,
linger and loiter in the back,
between the magazine and comic book racks,
until old man Shoop would shout,
tell us to go on and get out,
send us flying up High Street
past the churches and the old ladies crying, "Oops!"

Or prisoners in Spring, leaning
from the second-story windows of the old county jail,
pushing tattooed arms through the iron bars,
sending cigarette smoke aloft in skinny, ecclesiastical
            trails,
calling out to the Catholic school children passing
            below,
"Don't do like me! You'll hate to go!"
or again, "Come a little closer, kid! I'll eat you up!"
sending us fleeing along the railroad tracks,
into the woods behind the housing tracts,
where fast away in plywood forts we cut
and inked our arms in secret signs,
and kneeling bare-chested in the dappled moonlight,
puked up our guts on sweet Thunderbird wine.

Robert Anbian has worked as a journalist, editor, political consultant, book and film critic, corporate publicist, and propagandist for left-wing causes. He's also been a plumber, roofer, pizza delivery guy, bartender, draft dodger, subject of government drug study, and Africa Peace Corps volunteer. "Where the road ends the road goes on."